THE QUICK & EASY GUIDE TO STARTING YOUR FIRST PODCAST

The Quick & Easy Guide to Starting Your First Podcast

B. Vincent

QuillQuest Publishers

Contents

Introduction

Welcome to "The Speedy and Simple Manual for Beginning Your First Webcast," your extensive guide to sending off a fruitful digital recording without any preparation. Whether you're an excited narrator, an enthusiastic master in your field, or somebody hoping to make a computerized space for conversation and local area constructing, this guide is for you.

Podcasting has detonated in ubiquity throughout recent years, offering a phenomenal stage for voices, everything being equal, to be heard all over the planet. With the obstructions to passage lower than at any other time, there could be no more excellent chance to begin your podcasting venture than now.

In this book, we'll walk you through each step of the cycle, from the underlying arranging stage to recording, altering, distributing, and then some. Our point is to demystify the universe of podcasting, separating the specialized angles into straightforward areas and furnishing you with reasonable exhortation to get your digital recording going.

What's in store

All through this aide, you'll track down nitty gritty directions, master tips, and noteworthy techniques to assist you with exploring the podcasting scene. We'll cover:

•Arranging Your Digital broadcast: All that you really want to consider prior to stirring things up around town button, including picking a point, characterizing your crowd, and defining your objectives.

•The Specialized Essentials: A direct gander at the gear and programming you'll require, in addition to guidance on setting up your recording climate.

•Content Creation: Methods for making drawing in, convincing substance that will make your audience members want more and more.

•Recording and Altering: A bit by bit manual for creating top notch digital broadcast episodes, including a prologue to altering procedures.

•Distributing and Advertising: How to get your webcast out into the world and guarantee it tracks down its crowd.

•Adaptation and Development: Procedures for transforming your webcast into a productive endeavor and growing your arrive at over the long run.

An Expression of Consolation

Beginning a digital broadcast can appear to be overwhelming, particularly in the event that you're new to sound creation. Yet, recollect, each extraordinary podcaster began precisely where you are presently. With energy, commitment, and the direction gave in this book, you'll be well headed to making a webcast that resounds with audience members and hangs out in the swarmed podcasting space.

We have faith in you and your podcasting venture. How about we leave on this interesting experience together.

1

Chapter 1: Understanding Podcasting

Podcasting: A Cutting edge Story of Correspondence

Podcasting, a portmanteau of "iPod" and "broadcasting," has developed a long ways past its starting points to turn into a critical mode for narrating, schooling, and diversion. This development can be followed back to the mid 2000s when the first digital recordings started to show up. The straightforwardness of making and conveying sound substance considered a different scope of voices to find a group of people outside customary media channels.

The Flood of Prevalence

The genuine flood in podcasting's prominence, be that as it may, accompanied the approach of cell phones and versatile web access. This mechanical jump made web recordings promptly available to a worldwide crowd, changing drives, exercise meetings, and even family tasks into potential open doors for learning, diversion, and self-awareness.

Why Podcasting?

The allure of podcasting lies in its adaptability and closeness. Web recordings can take special care of practically any interest, from the complexities of quantum material science to the everyday existences of individuals living in various regions of the planet. This far reaching content is conveyed in a configuration that feels individual, frequently making a feeling of one-on-one discussion between the host and the audience.

Advantages of Beginning a Digital recording

Beginning a digital recording offers various advantages, both individual and expert. Here are a few key benefits:

1. Voice to Your Energy: Podcasting gives a stage to impart your enthusiasm to the world, whether it's narrating, a particular side interest, or an expert field.
2. Building a Local area: By sharing your inclinations, you draw in similar people, making a local area of audience members who share your interests.
3. Networking Open doors: Facilitating a digital recording can open ways to discussions with specialists, powerhouses, and other podcasters, extending your expert organization.
4. Skill Turn of events: The method involved with making a webcast improves different abilities, including sound creation, narrating, and research.
5. Monetization Potential: Effective digital recordings can create pay through promoting, sponsorships, and audience support.

Understanding the embodiment of podcasting and its advantages is the most important move toward making your own digital recording. This section has established the groundwork by investigating the medium's set of experiences, its ascent in prevalence, and the extraordinary benefits it offers to content makers. As we push ahead, remember these advantages as we dive into the preparation, creation, and development of your digital broadcast.

2

Chapter 2: Planning Your Podcast

Picking Your Web recording Point

Choosing a point for your digital recording could appear to be overwhelming from the get go, yet everything revolves around offsetting energy with request. Here are a few hints to direct your decision:

1. Follow Your Inclinations: Begin with what you love. A subject you're energetic about will keep you persuaded, particularly whenever difficulties arise.
2. Identify a Specialty: While it's enticing to take care of expansive interests, specialty themes frequently draw in committed crowds. Find an exceptional point or viewpoint that sets your digital broadcast separated.
3. Consider Your Mastery: Utilizing your expert or individual aptitude can enhance your digital broadcast, situating you as an expert in your field.

Characterizing Your Interest group

Understanding who you're addressing is all around as significant as understanding what you'll talk about. This is the way to characterize your main interest group:

1. Create Audience Personas: Envision your optimal audience. Think about their age, interests, calling, and what questions they could need your web recording to reply.
2. Research Existing Crowds: Take a gander at comparative digital recordings and their crowds. Virtual entertainment stages and gatherings can likewise give bits of knowledge into possible audience members' inclinations and trouble spots.
3. Engagement: Plan how you will draw in with your crowd. Will you utilize virtual entertainment, email pamphlets, or direct collaboration through audience call-ins or back and forth discussions?

Defining Digital recording Objectives

Clear objectives give guidance and assist with estimating achievement. Think about these goals:

1. Educational or Diversion Worth: Choose if your digital recording expects to teach, engage, or both. This choice will shape your substance and show style.
2. Audience Development: Set reasonable focuses for crowd development. Utilize these to direct your promoting and content systems.
3. Monetization: On the off chance that adaptation is an objective, ponder when and how you could present sponsorships, promotions, or endorser just happy.

The arranging stage is basic in your podcasting venture. A very much picked subject that invigorates you, a plainly characterized crowd, and explicit objectives prepare for an effective web recording. As you push ahead, remember these components — they will impact each choice, from content creation to showcasing and adaptation methodologies.

3

Chapter 3: The Technical Basics

Fundamental Podcasting Gear

Beginning a digital recording doesn't need an expert studio, yet a couple of key bits of hardware are fundamental for creating clear, captivating substance. You'll require this:

1. Microphone: The foundation of your arrangement. A decent quality mouthpiece can fundamentally upgrade your sound quality. Think about USB mouthpieces for convenience or XLR amplifiers for better sound quality assuming that you're willing than put resources into a sound connection point.

2. Headphones: For observing your sound progressively. Shut back earphones are liked for podcasting to limit sound break.

3. Recording Programming: There are numerous advanced sound workstation (DAW) choices accessible, going from free programming like Boldness to proficient grade applications

like Adobe Tryout. Pick one that accommodates your financial plan and intricacy level.

Setting Up Your Recording Space
Your recording climate assumes a critical part in the sound quality. Here are a few hints to improve your space:

1. Minimize Reverberation: Record in a little, covered room with drapes and upholstered furniture to diminish reverberation. If conceivable, utilize acoustic boards or froth to hose sound reflections.
2. Control Foundation Commotion: Pick a calm general setting to record. Straightforward marks like switching off fans or cooling during recording can have a major effect.
3. Proper Receiver Strategy: Position the receiver accurately — about a clench hand's separation from your mouth — and talk straightforwardly into it for the best solid quality.

Recording and Altering Programming
While recording programming catches your sound, altering programming is where you'll invest energy cleaning your accounts. Key elements to search for include:

1. Multi-track Altering: Empowers you to layer different sound tracks, like music, audio cues, and voice, for a more powerful listening experience.
2. Noise Decrease: Valuable for tidying up foundation clamor or murmur in your accounts.
3. Equalization and Pressure: Instruments to adjust your sound levels and guarantee a steady volume across episodes.

Understanding the specialized nuts and bolts of podcasting sets the establishment for delivering excellent sound substance. Putting resources into the right hardware and figuring out how to advance your recording climate and programming can lift your digital broadcast from beginner to proficient. Keep in mind, the objective is to give an unmistakable, wonderful listening experience for your crowd, guaranteeing they center around your substance as opposed to any sound interruptions.

4

Chapter 4: Content Creation

Creating Drawing in Happy

The way in to a fruitful digital broadcast is content that dazzles and enhances your audience members. This is the way to guarantee your substance sticks out:

1. Consistency is Critical: Lay out a steady topic and tone for your digital broadcast. This helps set audience assumptions and constructs a dependable crowd.
2. Know Your Crowd: Designer your substance to meet the interests and needs of your characterized crowd. Input and commitment measurements can direct happy changes.
3. Diverse Configurations: Trial with various episode designs, like independent critique, interviews, back and forth discussions, or narrating, to keep your substance new and locking in.

Organizing Your Episodes

A very much organized episode upgrades audience experience and maintenance. Think about the accompanying construction as a beginning stage:

1. Introduction: Momentarily present yourself, your web recording, and the episode's subject. This makes way for the episode.
2. Main Substance: Convey the main part of your substance here, whether it's an inside and out conversation, interview, or story. Keep it engaged and locking in.
3. Call-to-Activity: Urge audience members to buy in, share, or draw in with your digital recording via web-based entertainment. This can likewise incorporate advancing your site or product.
4. Outro: Finish up with a concise synopsis of the episode and bother the substance of the following episode to make audience members want more.

Methods for Narrating and Talking

Convincing narrating and successful talking can essentially improve your digital broadcast's allure. Here are a few hints:

•For Narrating:

oUse clear portrayals and individual stories to make a visual picture for your audience members.

oStructure your accounts with an unmistakable start, center, and end.

oUse stops and fluctuate your talking speed to construct anticipation and keep audience members locked in.

•For Talking:

oResearch your visitor completely to pose clever inquiries that uncover new features of their story or mastery.

oListen effectively and digress from your arranged inquiries in light of the discussion stream.

oEncourage visitors to share individual stories and bits of knowledge, as these minutes frequently reverberate most with audience members.

Making content for your digital recording includes a mix of imagination, arranging, and comprehension of your crowd. By zeroing in on conveying esteem through drawing in narrating and sagacious meetings, you can fabricate areas of strength for a, audience base. Keep in mind, the best happy mirrors your energy and uniqueness as a podcaster.

5

Chapter 5: Recording & Editing

Setting In the mood for Recording

Establishing a helpful recording climate and utilizing the right hardware are fundamental to catching quality sound. Here are a few key contemplations:

1. Quiet Climate: Pick a peaceful, very much protected space to limit foundation clamor. Wardrobes or rooms with delicate goods can function admirably.

2. Microphone Arrangement: Put resources into a decent quality receiver. Position it accurately to catch clear sound while diminishing pops and sibilance.

3. Recording Programming: Select a recording programming that suits your requirements. Numerous quality choices are accessible, going from free to proficient grade. Find out more about your product's fundamental capabilities prior to recording.

Recording Your Most memorable Episode

With your arrangement prepared, now is the ideal time to record your most memorable episode. Follow these means for a smooth recording meeting:

1. Script or Diagram: Set up an itemized layout or content. This guarantees you cover every one of your focuses while taking into account regular stream and suddenness.
2. Sound Check: Direct a sound check to change levels and guarantee your voice is unmistakable and at a fitting volume.
3. Record in Segments: Think about keep your episode in areas. This makes it simpler to oversee and alter, particularly for longer episodes.

Prologue to Altering

Altering is where you refine your recording into a cleaned episode. Fundamental altering abilities can essentially improve your digital broadcast's quality.

1. Choosing Altering Programming: There are various altering programming choices accessible, from fledgling well disposed to cutting edge. Search for programming with a decent arrangement of fundamental altering devices and an easy to use interface.
2. Basic Altering Strategies:

oTrimming: Eliminate undesirable segments all along, center, or end of your recording.

oNoise Decrease: Use sound decrease instruments to limit foundation clamor.

oLevel Change: Change the volume of your tracks for consistency and lucidity all through the episode.

oAdding Music and Impacts: Acquaint music or audio effects with improve the listening experience. Guarantee you reserve the privileges to utilize any music or impacts in your web recording.

Best Practices for Altering

•Enjoy Reprieves: Altering can be drawn-out. Enjoy normal reprieves to keep a new viewpoint on your substance.

•Use Earphones: Alter with great quality earphones to get un-obtrusive sound issues you could miss on speakers.

•Look for Input: Prior to settling your episode, get criticism from somebody you trust. New ears can get issues you could have disregarded.

Recording and altering are basic strides in webcast creation, changing your substance from crude sound to a firm, captivating episode. While the expectation to absorb information can be steep, fostering these abilities will essentially improve the nature of your digital broadcast. Keep in mind, practice and persistence are key as you refine your cycle after some time.

6

Chapter 6: Publishing Your Podcast

Picking a Digital broadcast Facilitating Stage

Before your digital broadcast can arrive at audience members' ears, you really want a spot to store and circulate your sound records. A webcast facilitating stage fills this need. This is the way to choose one:

1. Storage and Data transmission: Survey the extra room and transfer speed the stage offers. Guarantee it can oblige your digital recording's document sizes and audience numbers.
2. Distribution: Search for facilitating stages that offer simple dissemination to major web recording registries like Apple Digital broadcasts, Spotify, and Google Digital broadcasts.
3. Analytics: Pick a stage that gives point by point examination. Understanding your crowd's way of behaving is urgent for development and improvement.

4. Cost: Think about your financial plan. There are both free
and paid facilitating administrations, each with their upsides
and downsides. Figure out the thing highlights merit putting
resources into for your digital broadcast's prosperity.

Dispersing Your Web recording

With your facilitating stage chosen, the following stage is con-
veyance. This is the way to augment your web recording's range:

1. Submit to Digital broadcast Indexes: Physically present your
webcast to famous catalogs. This incorporates Apple Webcasts, Spotify, Google Digital broadcasts, and any specialty
indexes applicable to your crowd.
2. Promote via Web-based Entertainment: Utilize your own
and digital broadcast's virtual entertainment records to report
new episodes and draw in with your crowd.
3. Leverage Your Organization: Support companions, family,
and expert contacts to tune in and share your webcast.

Grasping RSS Channels

A RSS (Truly Basic Partnership) channel is a vital part of webcast
dissemination. It permits digital recording registries to naturally re-
fresh when you discharge new episodes. This is the thing you want
to be aware:

1. Automatic Updates: Whenever you've presented your digital
broadcast's RSS channel to a registry, new episodes will con-
sequently show up in the catalog when you distribute them
on your facilitating stage.
2. One-Time Arrangement: Setting up your RSS channel is
regularly a one-time process. Most facilitating stages will

create a RSS channel for you, which you can then submit to different registries.

3. Essential Data: Your RSS channel contains crucial data about your digital recording, including episode titles, portrayals, and the sound documents themselves. Guarantee this data is exact and refreshed in your facilitating stage.

Distributing your digital broadcast is a basic move toward contacting your crowd. By choosing the right facilitating stage, circulating your digital broadcast across different channels, and understanding the mechanics of RSS channels, you set up for your webcast's prosperity. With your episodes now open, you can zero in on developing your crowd and drawing in with your audience members.

7

Chapter 7: Marketing Your Podcast

Building a Web-based Presence

Your digital recording's web-based presence stretches out past the sound episodes. A solid, durable web-based personality assists audience members with finding, perceive, and interface with your digital broadcast.

1. Create a Site: Your digital broadcast's site is a focal center for everything connected with your show. Incorporate episode chronicles, show notes, about the host(s) page, and contact data. Website design enhancement streamlining is critical to making your webpage discoverable.

2. Email Pamphlets: An email list permits direct correspondence with your audience members. Share episode refreshes, in the background content, and select proposals to keep your crowd locked in.

Utilizing Web-based Entertainment

Web-based entertainment stages are important devices for web recording showcasing, permitting you to arrive at potential audience members where they invest a lot of energy.

1. Choose the Right Stages: Spotlight on stages where your interest group is generally dynamic. Instagram, Twitter, Facebook, and LinkedIn each have one of a kind qualities and crowd socioeconomics.

2. Content Technique: Make a blend of content kinds (text, pictures, recordings) to advance your episodes, share significant data, and draw in with your crowd. Use planning instruments to keep a reliable posting beat.

3. Engagement: Effectively draw in with your devotees. Answer remarks, partake in applicable discussions, and team up with other podcasters or powerhouses in your specialty.

Drawing in with Your Crowd

Building a local area around your web recording cultivates faithfulness as well as energizes informal exchange advancement.

1. Listener Criticism: Urge audience members to leave audits and input. Besides the fact that this gives significant bits of knowledge to progress, yet certain audits likewise help your digital recording's perceivability on stages.

2. Interactive Components: Consolidate audience questions, whoops, or voice message messages into your episodes. This intuitive component causes your crowd to feel esteemed and part of your webcast's local area.

3. Live Occasions and Meetups: Contingent upon your digital recording's degree and crowd size, consider facilitating live occasions or meetups. These can be incredible open doors for

developing associations with your most drawn in audience members.

Showcasing your web recording is a continuous exertion that assumes an essential part in your digital broadcast's development and achievement. By building areas of strength for a presence, utilizing web-based entertainment really, and connecting straightforwardly with your crowd, you can expand your perceivability and draw in additional audience members. Keep in mind, consistency and veritable communication are critical to building a dedicated audience base.

8

Chapter 8: Monetizing Your Podcast

Figuring out Adaptation

Prior to jumping into explicit techniques, it's essential to perceive that adaptation ought to line up with your web recording's substance, crowd, and values. Fruitful adaptation regularly requires a strong audience base, so center first around making important substance and connecting with your crowd.

Associations and Sponsorships

Sponsorships are a pervasive type of webcast adaptation, including concurrences with organizations to advance their items or administrations on your show.

1. Finding Supporters: Search for organizations whose items or administrations line up with your digital recording's subject and crowd interests. You can likewise join webcast promoting networks that associate digital broadcasts with expected supports.

2. Sponsorship Models: Sponsorships can be founded on a level charge, the quantity of downloads, or member showcasing, where you procure a commission for each deal made through a promotion code or connection gave in your digital recording.

Enrollment Models

Offering restrictive substance or advantages to paid supporters is a viable method for adapting your digital recording while at the same time encouraging a nearer local area.

1. Subscription Administrations: Stages like Patreon permit podcasters to offer different membership levels, conceding admittance to selective episodes, in the background content, or early episode discharges.
2. Value Suggestion: Guarantee that the elite substance or advantages you offer genuine benefit to your supporters. This could incorporate promotion free episodes, reward content, or admittance to a confidential local area or occasions.

Promoting

Selling marked product can be a rewarding income stream while likewise advancing your web recording.

1. Product Determination: Pick stock that reverberates with your crowd and mirrors your digital recording's personality. Well known choices incorporate shirts, mugs, stickers, and advanced items like digital books or courses.
2. E-trade Stages: Use online stages that represent considerable authority in stock for content makers. These administrations frequently handle creation, deals, and delivery, diminishing the responsibility on podcasters.

Extra Income Streams

•Live Shows: Facilitating live digital broadcast accounts can create pay through ticket deals and proposition a novel encounter to your crowd.

•Crowdfunding: For explicit undertakings or upgrades to your digital recording, crowdfunding efforts can give the essential assets while expanding audience contribution.

Adapting your digital broadcast requires a mix of imagination, crowd understanding, and vital preparation. While few out of every odd adaptation system will suit each web recording, investigating various choices can assist you with tracking down the best fit for your show. Keep in mind, the essential spotlight ought to continuously be on conveying worth to your audience members, with adaptation serving to help and upgrade your webcast's main goal.

9

Chapter 9: Scaling and Growing

Breaking down Audience Criticism

Input from your crowd is important for understanding what works and what doesn't. This is the way to involve this data for development:

1. Surveys and Web-based Entertainment: Routinely request input through overviews or online entertainment stages. Pose explicit inquiries about what audience members appreciate and what they might want to see moved along.
2. Analytics: Use webcast facilitating and examination apparatuses to follow audience commitment, episode fame, and segment data. This information assists tailor with satisfying to your crowd's inclinations.
3. Adapt and Develop: Use criticism and examination to present new fragments, change episode arranges, or investigate points

that resound with your crowd. Remaining versatile is vital to keeping your substance new and locking in.

Extending Your Digital recording's Span
To become your digital broadcast, you really want to ceaselessly search for ways of arriving at new audience members. Think about these techniques:

1. Cross-Advancement: Team up with other podcasters to advance each other's shows. This can be through visitor appearances, online entertainment whoops, or shared content.
2. SEO for Webcasts: Streamline your digital recording's site and content for web crawlers. Utilize pertinent watchwords in your show notes and blog entries to draw in natural rush hour gridlock.
3. Utilize Different Stages: Circulate your web recording across however many stages as would be prudent. Every stage has its own crowd, expanding your possibilities of disclosure.

Working together with Powerhouses and Specialists
Coordinated efforts can acquaint your digital recording with new crowds and add an incentive for existing audience members.

1. Guest Appearances: Welcome specialists, forces to be reckoned with, or famous characters as visitors on your web recording. This enhances your substance as well as draw in their adherents to your show.
2. Participate in Podcasting People group: Draw in with podcasting networks on stages like Reddit, Friction, or Clubhouse. These people group can offer help, guidance, and open doors for cross-advancement.

3. Attend Podcasting Gatherings: Meetings and meetups are
   fantastic for systems administration with other podcasters
   and industry experts. They can prompt joint efforts, sponsorships, and other learning experiences.

Scaling and becoming your webcast is a continuous cycle that requires persistence, perseverance, and a readiness to adjust to your crowd's evolving needs. By zeroing in on audience criticism, extending your compass, and teaming up with others in the business, you can keep on building your digital broadcast's prosperity over the long run. Keep in mind, the excursion of podcasting is long distance race, not a run, and each step you take towards development adds to the bigger story of your web recording.

Conclusion: Embarking on Your Podcasting Journey

The Pith of Podcasting

At its center, podcasting is tied in with sharing stories, information, and interests with the world. A medium takes into consideration individual articulation and association with a worldwide crowd. All through this aide, we've investigated not just the specialized and key parts of beginning and growing a digital recording yet additionally the enthusiasm and commitment expected to make it effective.

Key Focal points

1. Planning Is Principal: A very much arranged digital recording has a superior potential for success of progress. From picking a point and characterizing your crowd to laying out clear objectives, the arranging stage sets the establishment for all that follows.

2. Quality written substance is the final deciding factor: Drawing in, significant substance will keep your crowd returning many episodes. Whether through narrating, interviews, or instructive substance, consistently endeavor to enhance your audience members' lives.

3. Technical Capability: Figuring out the specialized fundamentals — from recording hardware to altering programming —

is significant. In any case, recall that flawlessness accompanies practice, and your abilities will work on over the long run.

4. Consistent Commitment: Building and keeping a group of people requires steady exertion in making content, advertising your digital broadcast, and drawing in with your audience members. Your crowd is the core of your webcast; support this relationship.

5. Growth Is an Excursion: Scaling and becoming your webcast includes tolerance, variation, and progressing learning. Embrace input, look for joint efforts, and consistently search for ways of arriving at new audience members.

Last Uplifting statements

Beginning your first digital recording is an astonishing undertaking loaded up with potential and conceivable outcomes. As you set out on this excursion, recollect that each effective podcaster began precisely where you are currently. The way might have its difficulties, yet the awards of associating with a crowd of people and it are unlimited to share your enthusiasm.

Allow this manual for be your guide, yet additionally trust in your imagination and impulses. The podcasting scene is improved by variety and development, and there's consistently space for new voices and thoughts.

Remain inquisitive, remain energetic, and let the world hear what you need to say. Your podcasting experience starts now.

www.ingramcontent.com/pod-product-compliance
Lightning Source LLC
Chambersburg PA
CBHW030238150726
47988CB00021B/3323